PRACTICAL MEDITATION describes the methods and spiritual knowledge of Raja Yoga as taught by the Brahma Kumaris World Spiritual University, Mt Abu, Rajasthan.

Each chapter explores a basic aspect of Raja Yoga meditation, explaining deep concepts in simple language. All chapters finish with a short meditation commentary.

practical meditation

Practical Meditation

First Edition November 1988
Second Edition July 1989
Third Edition January 1994
Fourth Edition April 1997

Available in other languages

ISBN 0-9592271 1 3

This book has been produced by The Brahma Kumaris World Spiritual University, a
non-profit organisation, with the aim to share spiritual knowledge as a community
service for the personal growth of individuals.
The Brahma Kumaris World Spiritual University (BKWSU) exists to serve the family
of humanity; to assist individuals to discover and experience their own spirituality
and personal growth; to understand the significance and consequences of individual
action and global interactions; and to reconnect and strengthen their eternal
relationship with the Supreme Soul, the spiritual parent.

Contents

Lesson 1

Why meditation?

People want a variety of things from meditation. Some come for peace, others for control; some for power and some for silence; but of all the reasons, the one which is most often expressed is peace, or peace of mind. At first there doesn't seem to be much difference between the two; but on closer inspection we find that they are asking for different things. Peace is simply an experience, whereas peace of mind is a way of life.

At some time or other we have all enjoyed a moment's peace, however fleeting. Simply to experience peace is not actually so difficult. Peace is something easily attainable through the practice of meditation because this is what meditation is specifically designed to give. However, to attain peace of mind implies that I want to experience peace constantly. While I go about my daily life, I need to be in control of myself to the extent that I can have whatever experience I choose when I choose. To experience constant peace of mind, I need something more than just a meditation technique. After all, in the middle of a dispute with the bus conductor over the change, I can't just sit myself down and spend five minutes delving into the deep recesses of the self to regain that temporarily lost inner peace! It is the experience of peace, previously gained through meditation, which I need to be able to use later on in my practical life, especially at times when it is not easy to be peaceful. If I can't use my meditation to bring benefit into my daily life, is it really of any use to me?

Therefore, the emphasis in this meditation course will be a double one.

Firstly, to teach a simple, effective method of meditation called Raja Yoga, and to discuss and experiment with ideas on how to deepen the experiences gained.

Secondly, to look at the reasons behind stress and tension in my life, so that through understanding I can begin to change the root causes, using the power gained through meditation; and also, to clarify how I can translate peaceful feelings into peaceful actions, so that peace becomes peace of mind.

WHAT IS MEDITATION?

Meditation is the process of getting to know myself completely: both who I am 'inside' and how I react to what is 'outside'. Above all, meditation is 'enjoying myself' in the literal sense. Through meditation, I discover a very different 'me' from the stressed or troubled person who may seem superficially to be 'me'. I realise that my true nature, the real me, is actually very positive. I begin to discover an ocean of peace right here on my own doorstep.

There is a lovely Indian story about a queen who had lost her valuable pearl necklace. In great distress, she looked everywhere for it; and just when she was about to give up all hope of ever finding it she stopped and realised it was right there around her own neck! Peace is very much like this. If I look for it outside in my physical surroundings or in other people, I will always be disappointed; but if I learn where and how to look for peace within myself, I will find that it has been here all the time.

The word 'meditation' is used to describe a number of different uses of the mind, from contemplation and concentration to devotion and chanting. The word itself is probably derived from the same root as the Latin word 'mederi', meaning 'to heal'.

Meditation can certainly be looked on as a healing process, both emotionally and mentally, and to a certain extent, physically too. The simplest definition of meditation is: the right use of the mind or positive thinking. It is not to deny thoughts, but to use them correctly. Most forms of meditation employ two main practices:

• concentration exercises, often using an object such as a
    mandala (picture based on a circular motif) or a flower or a
candle; and

• the repetition of a mantra.

A mantra is a sacred phrase, word or sound which is repeated constantly, either loudly, silently or in thoughts only. It translates literally as 'man' – 'mind' and 'tra' – 'to free'; so, 'that which frees the mind'. Raja Yoga meditation does involve concentration, but no physical object is involved. The object of concentration is the 'inner' self. Instead of repeating one word or phrase, as in a mantra, a flow of thoughts is encouraged, thus using the mind in a natural way.

This positive flow of thoughts is based on an accurate understanding of the self and so acts as a key to unlock the treasure trove of peaceful experiences lying within.

Sit in a comfortable position with the back straight. You can either sit on a cushion on the floor cross-legged or, if this is uncomfortable, sit on a chair. Choose a quiet place away from noise or visual distraction. Gentle background music may be played, as this helps to create a relaxed, light atmosphere.

Position the book in front of you and read the following meditation slowly and silently. Aim to experience and visualise the words in your mind so that you begin to feel what is being described.

THOUGHTS FOR MEDITATION

Let me imagine that nothing exists outside this room... I feel completely insulated from the outside world and free to explore my inner world... I turn all my attention inward, concentrating my thought energy on the centre of the forehead... I feel a sense of detachment from my physical body and the physical surroundings... I become aware of the stillness around me and within me... A feeling of natural peacefulness begins to steal over me... Waves of peace gently wash over me, removing any restlessness and tension from my mind... I concentrate on this feeling of deep peace,... just peace... I... am... peace... Peace is my true state of being... My mind becomes very calm and clear... I feel easy and content... having returned to my natural consciousness of peace... I sit for a while, enjoying this feeling of calmness and serenity...

Plan to practise repeating these or similar thoughts to yourself for about ten minutes at least twice a day. The best time is in the morning after a wash or shower, before you begin your day's activities. Another good time is in the evening, when your day's activities are over. During the day, while performing any activities, keep reminding yourself, 'peace is my true nature'.

As you keep practising this meditation, positive and peaceful thoughts will arise in the mind more and more easily, and peace of mind will become increasingly natural.

Lesson 2

Who am I?

This simple question seems easy to answer at first. However, as soon as I start to think about it, I realise that giving my name or a description of my physical appearance does not describe the myriad thoughts, moods, actions and reactions which comprise myself and my life. Even a description of what I do becomes confusing because, every day, I wear so many different hats. I may start the day as a wife or a husband. At work I may become a secretary, a clerk or a teacher. At lunch I may meet a friend and in the evening an acquaintance. Which of these roles that I play is me?

In each role that I play a different facet of my personality emerges. Sometimes I feel that I have to play so many different and opposing roles that I no longer know what sort of person I am. When I meet my boss at a party or my parents and friends come to visit at the same time, I become confused as to how to behave. Not only have I fixed myself a special way of acting towards them, but in my mind I have also limited them to a certain role. I am only able to relate to them as 'my boss' or 'my parents', not as simply other human beings. Yet I am quite aware that my true identity is not defined by the role I play. How can I think of myself? Who am I really?

What is needed is something constant, safe and stable. We get up in the morning, look in the mirror, and we seem to be much the same as we were yesterday. But we all know that this is an illusion because gradually, over time, the body is declining; it is not stable or constant. In Raja Yoga, instead of adopting this obvious bodily identification, we start with our thoughts, awareness or consciousness and identify with that, because our thoughts are always there, whatever age we are. Their content may change but our ability to think does not.

First of all, I am a thinking, experiencing being. Thoughts are not something physical which I can experience with the physical senses. I cannot see, taste or touch a thought. Thoughts are not made up of matter or even brain cells. I am a spiritual being. All thoughts are generated from the light source of the soul not from the physical matter of the body or the brain. The terms 'self' or 'soul' are used to describe this point of light energy.

The point of light is the only form that cannot be destroyed. It is something so small that it cannot be divided. It is something without any physical dimension. I, the soul, am a subtle star, a point source of light energy and consciousness. This subtle form is the source of everything that I do – all thoughts, all words, all actions. Whatever I do or say, it is I, the soul, who is performing that action through my body. The soul is like a driver and the body is the car. To be in complete control, the driver has to sit in the place where he has access to the controls and also can collect all the necessary information to make decisions. Each thought, leading to words and actions, begins with an impulse from the brain. In Raja Yoga it is considered that the soul is located behind the centre of the forehead in the brain. This third eye, the point of reference, helps focus my attention.

My fundamental identity is a soul, free of gender and role. All the other identities – teacher, student, man, woman, father, mother, friend, relation and so on – are simply different roles which I, the soul, play.

Good actors can play any role. They will play their roles to the best of their ability, but will never actually think: 'I am Hamlet' or 'I am Cleopatra'. They know that, however involved they are with their roles, at the end of the performance they will take off their costumes and resume their day-to-day identities. So, whatever role I, the soul, am required to play, I understand that my spiritual identity is as a soul – a living, eternal being. The body is simply my temporary physical costume.

The soul has innate, peaceful, positive qualities. In meditation I create an awareness of myself as a soul. This naturally leads to an experience of these peaceful, positive qualities. This is what is called 'soul-consciousness'. It is not just something to experience while in meditation, but also as I perform action. As I become more aware that it is 'I, the soul' who is performing each action, I gain greater control over my thoughts, feelings, words and actions. The natural consciousness of myself as a peaceful being then fills all my actions and the desire for peace of mind is fulfilled in a completely practical way.

In meditation I begin to think about my true identity. I let thoughts about the soul and its qualities fill my mind. Initially it doesn't matter how fast the thoughts are arising as long as they are moving in the right direction. If my thoughts wander away, gently I bring them back again to peaceful thoughts of the self. As I become involved in the experience of such thoughts, they will gradually start to slow down and soon I will be able to 'savour' them. Just as when I am given something special to eat, I eat it slowly, appreciating each mouthful for its flavour and texture, so I begin to appreciate the experience contained in each positive thought. The simple phrase, 'I am a peaceful soul', comes to life as I begin to experience it.

This is a very different approach to meditation from repeating a mantra or focusing on a candle or the rhythm of the breath. In Raja Yoga, sitting meditation is complemented by maintaining a peaceful soul-conscious state while performing everyday actions.

Through maintaining soul-consciousness in this way, I continue to progress towards my aim of attaining constant peace of mind. A mantra is used purely for sitting meditation. In Raja Yoga, however, I bring my thoughts in meditation directly into my daily life. This is the first and most important step in making meditation practical. As I go around doing things, I experience being a soul, acting a role through the body. My consciousness becomes detached from the body. When I see another human being, I look beyond the name, body, race, culture, sex or age and see, with the vision of equality, a soul, like myself, who is simply playing a different role. This helps develop the qualities needed to remain peaceful all the time, such as tolerance, patience and love.

Through understanding and experiencing my true qualities, I regain confidence and self-respect and am no longer pushed and pulled by the expectations of others. By remaining soul-conscious, I will stay in my true state of peace. This is something which does, of course, take time and patient effort to practise. The reward of practice is enjoyable in itself and the greater benefits will accumulate over time.

When you sit to meditate, choose the quietest place you can find, preferably in a room which you do not use very often. If this isn't possible, sit where the familiar objects around you won't distract your attention. Set this place aside, purely for the purpose of meditation. This mental preparation will help your concentration. Start with 10 or 15 minutes. This will gradually lengthen naturally with experience. Soft or subdued lighting will help. A meditation commentary tape can be used to guide the mind in a positive direction. These tapes are available from any Raja Yoga Centre.

When you finish your meditation, just take a moment to reflect on what you have experienced; note how your mood has changed. This will emphasise your experiences and help you to appreciate what you are gaining through meditation. One more suggestion of great benefit is: Don't just meditate when you feel like it. The greatest progress is possible at the time when you really don't want to meditate or when you feel you can't. That's the time when you need to meditate the most!

THOUGHTS FOR MEDITATION

These thoughts are only a suggestion. Create your own similar thoughts if you prefer. Any thoughts based on the awareness of the self as a soul are valid. Think slowly and aim to experience each thought before moving on...

I withdraw my attention away from my physical limbs and senses... I focus on myself... I am listening through these ears... I am looking through these eyes... I am behind these eyes... in the centre of the forehead,... an eternal spark of life energy... This life energy empowers the body... I am a non-physical being,... an eternal soul... I am the actor... This body is simply my costume... I focus my thoughts on the point in the centre of the forehead,... a tiny point of conscient light... I feel completely detached from the body,... peaceful and light... I am a star radiating light... I find deep peace and contentment within... I now know my true self,... an eternal, pure, peaceful soul... I am in the ocean of peace... All conflict finishes... A deep, deep silence comes over me... Om shanti.

'Om', 'I am', and 'shanti', 'peace': 'I am a peaceful soul'.

16

Lesson 3
Soul-consciousness

W hy should the thought, 'I am a peaceful soul', be any more beneficial to me than the thought, 'I am a body'? In the previous lesson it was mentioned that this thought allows me to become detached from the role that I play. It is important to understand what is meant by this word 'detached'. It does not mean distant or inward-looking to the point of isolation, where there is a breakdown in communication. Nor does it mean that I become an uncaring observer of what is going on. It simply means to have the consciousness of being an actor. I play my part with great enthusiasm and love, but I do not let the expectations, burdens and worries of outside situations or other people affect my own understanding of who I am, a peaceful being. In fact, the word most often used in conjunction with 'detached' is 'loving'. By being aware of myself as a soul I experience my natural qualities, so that the feelings I associate with detachment are not distaste or lack of concern, but peace, love and happiness.

How can soul-consciousness help me improve my attitude towards myself and others? We often have the habit of comparing ourselves to others, seeing ourselves in the light of what we consider to be their merits or demerits. This can sometimes lead to a feeling of hopelessness, self-criticism and other equally negative states of mind. Through the experience of soul-consciousness, I come to realise my own worth and stop comparing myself with others. Self-criticism is overcome as I experience my true positive qualities and nature. This leads not to a feeling of superiority, but to a feeling of stability and self-confidence. Doubts in the self are replaced by a deeper faith in myself.

If I understand that I am a peaceful soul, I understand that others must also be that. Through this awareness, I will be able to relate to them on purely equal terms; that is, with what can be called the vision of brotherhood. Sometimes actions are totally opposed to this vision. Someone may get angry with me and I feel threatened, replying sharply in return. Thus a heated argument can develop. This is a reflection of body-consciousness. Instead of primarily seeing the other as a peaceful soul, playing a part, I am seeing the part and thinking it is the other's true nature.

If, instead, I have the determined thought to see others as souls, I will respond very differently to their anger. I will see their anger as being something temporary and not intrinsic to their true nature. Instead of reacting angrily or being defensive, I will actually become detached or even giving. I can put myself, quite naturally, into the position of being able to help them. I will recognise that their anger is only to do with their own confusion. This positive attitude acts as protection for me; I then don't feel under attack. In addition, my stable, calm reaction will help to defuse the situation.

There are other ways in which soul-consciousness can help me to help others. One cannot give what one doesn't have oneself. When friends come to us in distress, often the most we can do is give sympathy. Although this is reassuring, it is not necessarily very helpful. When in trouble, what people need most is power and clarity. The situation has caused weakness and confusion in their minds, making it difficult for them to see things clearly. If my reaction and suggestions to them are not only sympathetic, but also filled with peace, power and practicality, they can take away with them not only comfort, but something which will be of positive value in helping them to solve their problems. A strong and uncluttered mind is needed for this.

Soul-consciousness also allows me to be natural in the company of others. This ease on my part helps them to relax, as they don't feel that I have expectations of them. With soul-consciousness I aim only to see the good in others, to see not just apparent virtues, but hidden ones as well. This, in turn, helps others to realise their own positive virtues and specialties. A deepening love and respect for other souls naturally develops as I recognise my spiritual kinship with them. There is the realisation that we are all part of one global family, sharing one world, one home.

MEDITATION PRACTICE

Meditation is being aware of my natural qualities. It is not a difficult thing. Nor is it something that I impose on myself. I can't force myself to meditate. In fact the more hard effort I put in, the less likely I am to experience anything. Too much hard concentration will create a headache, and instead of refreshment and relaxation, there will be tension.

The first step is simply to relax. Many people would consider being able to relax at will as quite an achievement in itself. In meditation, once I become relaxed, the worries and stress of everyday life dissolve and the mind is free to explore gentle themes. My world is a creation of my own mind. This is why I fill my thoughts with soul-consciousness; thinking about peace helps me to experience peace.

The more relaxed I am, the deeper that pleasant, restful feeling becomes, until I have reached a powerful state of meditation, enjoying the quietness which is emerging from within. As I progress, meditation becomes much more than a relaxation technique. The object is not just relaxation; it is to become a peaceful person, to fill myself completely with peace. The experience of peace, gained through simple relaxation, is a mere drop compared to the ocean of peace in which I can lose myself through meditation.

I keep my thoughts or themes very simple in meditation; just two or three carefully-chosen ones are enough. I repeat them gently, giving myself plenty of time to explore the feelings behind them; for example, 'Peace is just like sinking into a feather mattress...'; 'Lightness is like floating on a cloud...'; 'Love is a warm, golden glow inside my mind...'.

20

As I become more and more engrossed in such thoughts and experiences, I feel myself gradually letting go of all worldly thoughts and tensions, until I become light and free.

Now I have become soul-conscious, aware of my true nature. It is this lightness of consciousness which I want to bring into my everyday life, so that whatever problems and obstacles come in front of me, I deal with them easily and effectively.

THOUGHTS FOR MEDITATION

For the next few days just take up two or three simple themes or phrases, such as *'I am a peaceful soul'*, *'I am a being of light and love, spreading these feelings to others and the world'* and *'I am a subtle point of consciousness, so different from the physical body'*. Repeat these thoughts gently to yourself, allowing them to sink in more and more deeply until your thoughts and your feelings match each other. When this happens, the tension between what you think you should be doing and what you actually are doing disappears, and the soul feels content and full. In addition, practise seeing others as souls, seeing beyond the part to the actor who is playing the part.

Lesson 4
This thing called mind

S itting down and experiencing peace is one thing; actually using it to transform my life is quite another. A great deal goes on between the intention and the action, and sometimes I catch myself saying 'I didn't want to do that, but...' or 'Sorry, I didn't mean to say that'. To be in full control of my life I need not only to know, but also to understand the process through which an intention becomes an action.

For instance, a variety of raw materials goes into a car manufacturing plant: sheet metal, nuts and bolts, electrical wiring, paint and so on. These raw materials can be compared to my experiences and intentions. As the raw materials pass through the plant, they are processed and eventually emerge as cars. However, imagine that there is a consistent fault in the production process. I could set about repairing each car as it comes off the production line, but this would be time-consuming and hard work. It would also be very frustrating, as I would consider that the factory had not been built to produce faulty cars.

Similarly, changing my actions superficially will not bring about profound changes in my life. This can work to a limited extent but I will be continually faced by 'faulty' actions from the 'production line', and it will seem like very hard labour with not much reward. Instead, I need to check the raw materials of my experience and also become familiar with the 'production process' of my desires and actions. It is not enough for the engineer only to know approximately what happens on the factory floor. To repair a fault he needs a detailed working knowledge of everything that is going on. The better he understands the machinery, the better he is at identifying and repairing the fault. So, the more I understand about how I work, the easier it is for me to eliminate the actions which I don't want. Through meditation I am checking the raw materials, ensuring that only the best quality is used and making sure that nothing is in short supply.

So, what is the process of manufacture? The first and most obvious thing that comes between an intention and an action is a thought. Thoughts occur in the mind. In Raja Yoga the mind is not seen as a physical thing but as a faculty of the soul, and therefore, non-physical. Through the mind I imagine, think and form ideas and so cultivate emotions, desires and sensations. It is through this process that, in an instant, I can re-live a past experience, produce happiness or sadness, or take myself to the other side of the world.

When there is the thought 'I want a cup of tea', the relevant actions seem to follow automatically. However, is thought the only link between intention and action? What about the expression 'Think before you speak'? Undoubtedly there must be thought before I open my mouth, or nothing would emerge; so, what is meant here? There seems to be two aspects to thought. The first is the thought itself; the second is the awareness and understanding of that thought. It is the intellect which is used to understand the thoughts. Through this second faculty of the soul, I assess the value of what emerges in the mind. In the expression 'Think before you speak', I am being asked to use my intellect and consider whether my thoughts are worth uttering. Some other functions of the intellect are reasoning, realisation, discrimination, judgement and the exercise of will power.

The intellect is the most crucial faculty; through the intellect I exercise control over my mind and, thus, over myself. The purpose of meditation is to fill the intellect with power, so making me clear-headed and perceptive, as well as developing firm resolve. The intellect is recognised by the effect that it has. For instance, someone explains something and I fail to understand it. So he tries explaining it in three or four different ways, but still I don't understand. Finally, the fifth time, I 'see the light' or 'the penny drops', that is, I realise what he means. This realisation is the working of the intellect.

Another example might be the process through which I sort out a plan of action to take, when faced with a choice of two or three possibilities. I weigh up the advantages and disadvantages until my power of judgement tells me which plan is the most suitable. Like the mind, the intellect is a subtle non-physical thing and belongs to the soul, not the body.

There is a third faculty of the soul, which comprises the impressions left on the soul by actions we have performed. These impressions can be referred to by the Sanskrit word 'sanskaras', for which there is no simple translation. Habits, emotional tendencies, temperament, personality traits are all built up by sanskaras imprinted on the soul through each action it has performed. Sanskaras create the personality in the same way that individual frames on a feature film make up a story. Every action is recorded, whether it is a physical movement, a word or even a thought. As I live my life, I am making an imprint on the celluloid, the soul. All the thoughts that occur in the mind are due to the sanskaras. Personality, the most fundamental feature of each individual, unique soul, is determined by these sanskaras.

The mind, intellect and sanskaras function together in a cyclic pattern which determines how I behave, what thoughts I have and even what mood I am in. Firstly, the mind produces thoughts – evidence which the intellect judges. On the basis of that judgement, an action is performed or not performed. The action, or non-action, creates a sanskara which, in turn, becomes part of the evidence in the mind.

A good illustration of this is the formation of a habit such as smoking. The first time I am offered a cigarette many thoughts, both for and against, arise in the mind: 'It's bad for my health', 'I wonder what it tastes like', 'It is very easy to get addicted', 'Everyone else does it' and so on. On the basis of these thoughts, the intellect makes a decision. Let's suppose that it makes the decision to try a cigarette. A sanskara is created by that action and the next time I am offered a cigarette that previous action becomes part of the evidence in the mind as a memory: 'I smoked one before'. If I decide to smoke one again, the repetition deepens that sanskara, just like planing a groove in a piece of wood, until eventually the evidence in the mind, urging me to smoke, has become so overwhelming that no evidence for not smoking remains. The intellect has now ceased to exert its right of choice. There is no longer a choice or judgement to make. There is just the strong thought rising in the mind: 'Have a cigarette!' and I perform the action automatically. The intellect stands aside. I am no longer in control; my past actions as sanskaras are ruling my present.

However, I can also use this mechanism to create peaceful, positive sanskaras. As I sit in meditation, I experience myself as a peaceful soul. This experience forms a sanskara. The next time I am about to get angry, through force of habit the mind will present contrary evidence: 'I am a peaceful soul'. This forces the intellect to make a decision. As the intellect gains strength of will through meditation, it becomes easier to act on peaceful sanskaras, as opposed to negative sanskaras. Thus the intellect begins to control both the mind and actions. I, the soul, become the master of the present. I am no longer the slave of my past. Gradually, I reach a position where I choose to put into action only those thoughts which will lead me to experience permanent happiness and contentment.

MEDITATION PRACTICE

Take one aspect of yourself which you want to change. A few times a day create just one or two very powerful positive thoughts which will help change that negative habit or character trait. Do this with all the energy and enthusiasm you can muster. This will create a very powerful sanskara. When that positive thought for change comes into your mind again, it will bring with it the experience of enthusiasm. This will help you to put that intention into action at the appropriate time.

For example: if you want to give up the habit of criticising people, throughout the day keep creating the positive thought: *"I see all as peaceful souls. Instead of criticising their weaknesses, I will only see their virtues and specialties"*; or *"I must first change my own weaknesses before criticising the weaknesses of others"* .

Lesson 5
Keeping the balance

To continue to progress towards my aim of attaining constant peace of mind, the most important thing is balance. If a car is too heavily weighted on one side, the driver will find it difficult to control and manoeuvre. Problems will arise with the tyres, suspension and so on. The same can happen to me if I pay too much attention to sitting in meditation, being introverted, and not enough attention to relating peacefully to others. I may become withdrawn, living in my own inner world instead of the 'real world' outside. I may find that relationships with others become difficult.

There are four aspects to bear in mind to avoid such an imbalance. If equal weight is given to all four, I can remain balanced while making natural, easy progress. These four aspects are *knowing, being, becoming* and *giving*.

KNOWING REFERS TO THE STUDY OF KNOWLEDGE
I have been given the basic facts: I am a soul; my true nature is peaceful; I have a mind, intellect and sanskaras. Now I have to fit

them together. These facts are like the pieces of a jigsaw; it is only when they are fitted together in the correct way that the picture emerges. Each piece has a little bit of the pattern on it; on its own, it can only hint at what the completed picture is. By turning information over in my mind, playing with it, matching it up to life as it unfolds, I begin to create a coherent view of all events. Once there is understanding of the wider picture, I begin to feel that I am in control of my situation. When there is understanding, my intellect remains clear and I am able to act in a positive and effective manner. Knowledge allows me to be detached from potentially stressful situations.

BEING REFERS TO YOGA, THE EXPERIENCE OF MEDITATION

Even if I can identify the logical connections between bits of information which I have received, unless I have a grasp of the contexts in which they apply, their meaning, I cannot really say I have understood them. For instance, I could learn some simple phrases in Hungarian and be able to repeat them in the correct order; unless my teacher had explained the meanings of the words, the phrases would be of absolutely no use to me.

So, how am I to understand what words like 'peace', 'love', 'soul', 'detachment' mean? I understand these virtues only by experiencing them. The experience of peace makes 'peace' a reality. It also gives me a basis of trust and faith, for it is when the experience reinforces the idea that the soul can feel secure. This leads to trust in the knowledge; through that trust and sense of truth I build a stable foundation.

BECOMING REFERS TO MY ACTIONS

In the last paragraph, harmony between knowledge and experience was emphasised. If there is any contradiction, trust and stability disappear. Again, what is vital here is harmony between what happens internally and what happens externally. To sit in meditation and experience myself as a peaceful soul, and then immediately after meditation, to become angry with someone, renders that peaceful experience meaningless, and the soul feels lost and confused. Meditation must be made practical. Its positive power must be reflected in action. I will actually become that which I experience in meditation.

Putting the results of yoga into practice has, on the whole, to be a conscious thing. It won't happen miraculously, without my paying attention to it. It is easy to see why, if we again consider how the soul performs actions through the cycle of mind, intellect and sanskaras. Even though I am creating peaceful sanskaras in meditation, the old, angry sanskaras will continue to create negative thoughts in my mind, sometimes very powerfully. It is only through conscious choice within the intellect that I can discriminate and change my behaviour.

What is important to understand here is that I will never experience progress unless I make an effort actually to change my negative actions and habits. However good my experiences in meditation are, if they are constantly contradicted by my actions, I will continue to create negative thoughts about myself; my mind will become a battlefield instead of a haven of peace.

GIVING REFERS TO HARMONIOUS AND ALTRUISTIC RELATIONSHIPS WITH OTHERS

Although becoming peaceful myself automatically helps my relationships with others, I still have to pay attention to my relationships mainly because it is relationships with others that spark off peacelessness within myself. It is easy to be friendly and giving, when those around me are friendly and giving. Unfortunately, in today's world, we often find ourselves in interpersonal situations, ranging from mildly uncomfortable to openly hostile. In these situations the practice of giving is my protection. It protects me from experiencing negativity, but also benefits the other soul who is unfortunate enough to be feeling aggressive. I cannot give and receive at the same time; so, having the thought to spread only peace and good wishes means there is no room for responses of fear or resentment or the awakening of anger within myself.

These types of situations are the examinations which face me every day. It is how I cope in these instances which is the true test of my progress. When there is victory, I realise that I have truly understood some aspect of knowledge. If, however, I do become angry or get careless, the desire to 'get it right next time' sends me back to review the knowledge for deeper understanding. Sometimes I am in a position to help others directly by sharing my own positive experiences. When this happens, having put things in my own words makes me realise how much I have understood. Every time I return to the knowledge, I have moved forward a little bit. So, natural progress is taking place.

Giving should be done without the desire for return or reward. It should be a natural process, simply motivated by the wish to share with others positive experiences which have been internalised. Feeling happy and content is the natural reward of positive actions.

Without desires and expectations, giving becomes truly altruistic. When I have practised meditation for some time, giving becomes something beyond words. The knowledge and meditation experiences have become so much a part of me that simply by being my true positive self I give the experience of peace and virtue to others.

When all these four aspects of *knowing, being, becoming* and *giving* are in harmonious balance, the soul will be at peace with itself and in harmony with others. This state of practical soul-consciousness has been termed *'jeevanmukti'* or *'freedom in life'*.

MEDITATION PRACTICE

Slow down! Give yourself time to think before you act. Give your new peaceful sanskaras a chance to be put into practice. Give yourself permission to have the time to practise. Concentrate during the time you have available. Short periods of regular meditation will increase the benefit which you experience. Naturally, over time, the periods you remain in meditation will lengthen and the benefit will continue to increase.

Practise being detached from your own thoughts. Create the thought: *'I, the soul, am in the cinema, watching my thoughts come up on the screen of my mind'*. As you watch them, they will begin to slow down. Sort through them, discriminating between the positive and the negative or waste (ordinary) ones. Have action replays of the best thoughts and allow your thoughts to lead you into the experience which lies behind them.

If you find your mind is still too active or at all negative, first concentrate on that basic thought, 'I am a peaceful soul'. Observe the direction in which your thoughts flow from that positive source. Sometimes the mind will naturally go in a positive direction when you sit for meditation, but at other times it needs to be firmly steered and guided to avoid crashing into the rocks of negative emotions and thoughts!

Lesson 6

Karma

While I associated myself completely with my physical body, I did not realise that every action was having such a deep impact on me. Now, with the recognition of the self as a soul, I become aware that every single action is leaving an imprint, a record, which I carry with me eternally.

Up until now we human beings have found it very difficult to classify exactly what is right and what is wrong. Throughout history our definition of right and wrong has been fluctuating. Different cultures and religions came up with different definitions and classifications. Even within the same religion people of different generations have different ideas of right and wrong. Even if I don't consider the external situation at all, but look within myself, I find that my own understanding fluctuates a great deal. In childhood, my understanding was on one level; in adolescence it changed; in maturity it has changed yet again.

As I am being influenced by the atmosphere or the words of human beings, my intellect wavers in its judgement.

So, can I possibly arrive at a point where I know absolutely what is right and what is wrong? All my ideas, thoughts and judgement become coloured and, therefore, limited by this physical costume, the culture into which this body was born, as well as the limitations of gender and age. Only by maintaining the consciousness of my true identity, a peaceful soul, am I able to understand accurately what is right and wrong. This is simply because in soul-consciousness the soul can only experience peace, happiness and love. So it can only perform actions based on these qualities. These actions will be beneficial actions, bringing happiness and positive results.

In body-consciousness there is not the pure intention behind action. Our actions are performed with ulterior selfish motives such as greed, ego and possessiveness, and are therefore non-beneficial actions which give sorrow and bring negative results. So it is the consciousness with which we act that is important.

The Law of Karma, of action and reaction, is to the spiritual sphere what Newton's Law is to the physical world. It is absolute. It states: For every action there will be an equal and opposite reaction. 'Opposite', of course, means 'opposite in direction'. Whatever interactions I have with others, I receive the equivalent in return. This means that if I have given happiness, I will receive happiness in return; and if I have given sorrow, I will receive sorrow in return. The law is simple. When understood in its full depth, it can give insight into the significance of events in my own world and in the world at large.

In the Bible it is stated as: 'As you sow, so shall you reap'. This is also known as a law of cause and effect. Understanding this, when I see outcomes, I realise that outcomes occur only as a product of another event or cause.

Generally when I see the fruits of my karma, I tend to forget that I am responsible for the seed. If the fruit of karma is bitter, I often blame others for the taste and make them responsible for my suffering. Understanding the Law of Karma makes me take total responsibility for my own situation, my state of mind and indeed my whole life. So if there is a sorrowful outcome, I now understand that I have been responsible for the cause of sorrow.

Sometimes only half the Law of Karma is understood. People accept the effect of past actions on the present and deny the influence of actions on destiny, the unformed future. For example, a person may think: 'Whatever is happening to me now is because of my past actions; so there is nothing I can do about it. It is my fate'. This is incorrect. I can shape a very positive future now irrespective of my negative past actions. When I understand that I am responsible for my own situation, I will develop tolerance, acceptance and endurance – qualities which may have been missing before.

This 'other side' of the Law of Karma teaches that if I perform pure, beneficial actions, I can create a positive future in the direction of my choice. Not only am I not bound by fate, but the understanding of karma philosophy makes me the creator or master of my own destiny. This can be inspirational for others too. Karma refers to the activity. Destiny refers to the cumulative picture of many actions.

The negativity of the past has led me into 'karmic debts'. Where I have in the past given sorrow, I must now repay that debt by giving happiness. I have to settle 'karmic accounts'. However, just because I change my attitude doesn't necessarily mean others will change theirs. If I have courage and continue to give good wishes and perform pure actions in relation to other souls, gradually the karmic debts will be repaid. Then I can be free from the bondage of that debt.

The power to sustain this effort of settling past karmic debt comes through meditation or yoga. As I come to understand my own true nature more fully, I can understand that this is the true nature of everyone. I can see through the mask of negativity and relate to the soul directly. This will help me not to create further negative karma; I will not react badly to the negativity of others. With soul-consciousness I naturally give love and respect to others, and I will, in time, receive love and respect in return. Every action performed in soul-consciousness is an action through which I receive benefit, and thus, it benefits others.

Karma begins in the mind as thoughts – the seeds of action. As is the thought, so is the result. Thoughts, like actions, spread vibrations and influence the surrounding atmosphere. Karmically these vibrations will return.

Pure, peaceful, happy thoughts are the most valuable treasures of life. If I keep such beneficial thoughts in my consciousness wherever I go, I will create a pure atmosphere of peace and happiness, from which others will greatly benefit.

Understanding the consequences of actions means I take proper action. Having little control over my actions is a sure sign that I have little control over my mind. If I slow down, I give myself more time to do things properly. If something is well done, the likelihood is that it won't cause problems in the future. Jobs done in a rush often contain mistakes which have to be put right later, thereby causing more work. 'A good job well done' leaves me with a peaceful mind. A careless piece of work pulls my attention back to the poorly done task again and again. When I concentrate completely on what I am doing in the present, this allows me to be in full control of both mind and body. I keep performing actions in soul-consciousness so that no matter how much I have to do physically, I can remain light and peaceful.

MEDITATION PRACTICE

When sitting in meditation, take three positive qualities which follow on from each other, such as a) *stillness – silence – power* or b) *lightness – peace – contentment*. Take up each theme separately, creating thoughts that will lead you into the experience of each quality. Experience the first quality before moving on to the second, and the second before moving on to the third. For example, visualise a still pond in your mind's eye, ripple-free and motionless with only the movement of the breeze of your breath detectable. Then sense the unchallenged solitude of this mental posture, its reassuring silence and acceptance of its own state. Then move on to feel the increasing strength of knowing that no-one else can take away this sense of self. Become aware of your unassailable spirituality. In this way you can gently lead yourself into deeper experiences in meditation, as well as enjoy a variety of positive feelings and qualities.

Lesson 7
The Supreme

Throughout history, we human beings have sought many things. Above all we have desired two things: happiness and a perfect relationship. If we have achieved either one or both of these things, it has been a constant struggle to keep them. They have usually proven to be temporary. If we want to achieve them on a permanent basis, we must look beyond the limited gains of possessions, money and fragile human relationships.

Raja Yoga has two meanings: 'Sovereign Yoga' – the yoga through which I become the sovereign, the master of myself; and the 'Supreme Union', or 'Union with the Supreme'. This second aspect of Raja Yoga involves developing a relationship with the Supreme, the source of perfection, God. Within this yoga or union I can fulfil my wish for inner happiness and my desire for a perfect relationship.

It does not even require that I first believe in God. Simply an openness to the idea that there may be a greater source of spiritual energy than myself is useful. Through my own experiments with meditation I can develop an understanding of this idea. If someone asked me: 'Do you believe in the existence of Mr X?', I would be inclined to want to meet Mr X first, before committing myself. Under the circumstances, I would keep an open mind. Similarly, with the concept of a supreme spiritual energy, until there is direct experience, it would be unwise to commit oneself. Yet, if I want to have contact with the Supreme Being, there are certain things that I must know. Firstly, I should know the form of the Supreme so that I will be able to have accurate recognition. Secondly, I need to know what 'language' to use so that there can be communication. Thirdly, I need to know where our meeting can take place.

In Raja Yoga, just as we have a very precise notion of the form of the soul, so we also have a very precise notion of the form of the Supreme. In fact, the Supreme is recognised as the Supreme Soul. So, He has a form identical to that of the human soul – that is, a point source of consciousness, a spark of light energy.

When we use the word 'He', this is not to imply that we think of the Supreme as male. The soul itself has no gender; it is only the body which has gender. Whereas the human soul takes a body, the Supreme Soul never has a body of its own and so is neither male nor female.

God never enters the cycle of human birth and rebirth. So, He never forgets His original qualities, as we do. He remains eternally peaceful, blissful and powerful. Our memory of our original qualities becomes jaded by the process of rebirth.

God is eternally the unlimited ocean of virtues. He remains undepleted spiritually and so never needs anything. This means He

40

is totally benevolent, ever-giving. In fact, within Raja Yoga we have a particular name for the Supreme, and that is Shiv Baba. 'Shiv' means 'benevolent'. He is the only being who is truly altruistic, whereas we normally look for something in return, even if it is only the pleasure of giving. God gives without any desire or expectation of return. 'Baba' is a sweet and familiar name for 'father'; thus, 'Shiv Baba' is the 'benevolent Father' of all souls.

The reason 'Father' is used is because of the concept of a father giving an inheritance to his children. In this case, the inheritance received is peace, love, knowledge and happiness. The Supreme is also the Mother, the Friend and the Beloved. In fact, whatever relationship or positive role I wish to see in Him, I can, because He is the unlimited source of all qualities, both male and female. So, whatever the situation, I always have a source of help and strength to draw on, a source that is only a thought away.

How can I communicate with this being? Meditation is about experiencing myself, experiencing my own qualities. I create peaceful thoughts in order to experience peace. Paradoxically, the more I absorb myself in that peace, the fewer thoughts I need. The communication with the Supreme is on this level. I come to know Him through the experiences that I have of His qualities. I begin to feel those qualities surround me. My communication with God is primarily through silent experience. In deep silence I can lose myself in the Ocean of Peace. With this experience I feel refreshed. I begin to understand my own qualities and specialties more deeply, and this brings confidence. I take power, which enables me to maintain a peaceful stage, while going about my daily life.

I also need to know where to find Him. When I sit in meditation and go deep within myself, a feeling of stillness comes over me. In that silence, my experience is that I am in an unchanging world, a timeless world. Yet this physical world is ever-changing. If my consciousness is tied to the physical, I can never get away from the passage of time. It is as though I have taken my consciousness beyond this world to another world. We call this place the soul world, the original home of the soul. It is a timeless world of silence and stillness, full of peace and power, a world of infinite golden-red light. This is also the home of the Supreme Soul. Taking myself there, I begin to experience His unlimited qualities of peace, love, purity, bliss and power, surrounding me. Through this most perfect of all relationships, I take power and guidance so that I can clear my karmic debts of the past and create a peaceful, happy and stable future for myself.

MEDITATION PRACTICE
Sitting in a quiet and relaxed atmosphere, slowly read over the following thoughts about relationships with the Supreme Soul.

THOUGHTS FOR MEDITATION
When I meet the Supreme in the land beyond sound and movement, the only things that exist are the feelings in my heart... It is my open heart that God reads... He knows what it is I truly desire ... He fulfills that need... What is required of me is honesty, cleanliness and clarity in my own mind to enjoy fully this meeting with my Supreme Father... Baba... Baba fulfills my deepest needs and wishes in many ways through many

relationships... As the Father, God gives me love and understanding... As His child, I have the spiritual birthright to His inheritance, the unlimited treasure-store of all His perfect virtues and powers... I also experience the sweetness and comfort of God as the Mother, in whose lap the soul can rest in tenderness and care... I can share all my thoughts and hopes with Baba, my Friend, and even my doubts and problems, for there is nothing to hide from a true friend... I can enjoy a heart-to-heart conversation at any time I wish, in any place... Baba the Friend is always there...

As the Teacher, God fills me with truth... He has an answer for every question, advice for every need, revealing to the self all the secrets of time and eternity, unravelling the mysteries of creation, so that the meaning of life becomes so clear... for in God I have found the perfect teacher, the source of truth... And Baba is also my Liberator and Guide, freeing the self from all sorrows and suffering,... guiding me along the path to freedom and happiness... As my one Beloved, Baba is the Comforter of my heart... With Baba as my Beloved, the search for true love ends and the experience of contentment and completeness begins...

Having the experience of all these relationships with God provides me with everything I need,... fulfilling all my pure desires and dreams... The seed of all these relationships is love... Behind every thought and action of His is pure love and the wish only to bring benefit to the soul,... to uplift,... to purify me... God's love is unlimited and endless...

Lesson 8
Time waits for no one – or does it?

Sir Isaac Newton set up a picture of a world, ticking away inside a cosmic clock. Time was an absolute thing. A second was a second, no longer, no shorter. Wherever we are, in our living room or on a pulsar millions of light years away, whatever we are doing, time ticks away, independent of any outside influences. This is a 'common sense' view of time and, if we thought like this, we would be thinking along the same lines as Western scientists did for nearly 300 years after Newton.

Then, at the beginning of this century, Einstein presented a theory, the implications of which rocked the foundations of three centuries of work. This was the theory of relativity. Part of what Einstein said was that the only way one can measure time is by clocks, be they water clocks which drip every second or mechanical clocks which tick. Basically all clocks move and, therefore, time is dependent on movement; time is not totally independent. He wasn't the first person to think like this; he was, however, the first person to formulate a usable mathematical theory about it (containing that famous equation, $E = mc^2$). To understand this clearly, let's return to Newton's theories. What Newton said was that there is a cosmic clock out there ticking away, against which one can measure things. Time is passing by, independent of whatever is happening. Now let's do a little experiment. Imagine that we all go to sleep one night, and when we wake in the morning, everything is moving at half speed. According to Newton, 'real' time is still ticking away up there and, in fact, we are taking twice as long to do everything. In the final reckoning, a 'nine-to-five' job has not taken eight hours, but sixteen hours.

Einstein says that we have no way of knowing, when we wake up on the morning after this strange event, that everything is working at half its previous speed. There is no 'real' time there, by which to measure everything that happens. Time is a measure of our activities. If all the timepieces in the world have slowed down to half speed, then time itself has slowed down to half speed. In other words, Newton's time is rigid and Einstein's time is elastic.

When we woke up that morning, everything would have seemed normal. We wouldn't have felt that everything had slowed down, because the only way to judge that would have been by comparing it with something else which had not slowed down. In other words, things would still be moving at the same speed relative to each other.

How can these two ideas help me practically? Firstly, according to how I regard time, I am either its master or its servant. With a Newtonian outlook I become its servant, as 'time waits for no-one', and so I feel that I have to rush around, cramming as many activities as I can into every relentless second. Now, let us consider how it is more helpful to have Einstein's view of time.

In this case, time is dependent on rate of change. What is the changing thing within myself whose speed is going to govern how fast time appears to be moving? It is my own thoughts. If I slow my thoughts down, time will appear to expand. If I speed them up, time contracts. It's not that I slow my thoughts down in the same way I would slow down a record; I simply leave space between each thought or even between each word. I then become aware, not only of the thoughts, but also of the free spaces. Awareness of these peaceful spaces between thoughts brings me right into the present and gives me the feeling that there is 'room to manoeuvre', time to spare.

When I first approach something new, for instance, the first time I use a particular recipe, I read each instruction carefully. Then, thinking only about that, I perform the relevant action, returning to the cookery book again only after I have completed it. This mode of operation makes sure that everything is done correctly and the best possible result is attained. Having given myself time and space to do the job well, on completion of the task, I feel satisfied.

Compare this with the situation where the instructions, in the form of thoughts, follow each other in rapid succession, not waiting for each instruction to be put into action before the next one arises. The result is that, as I am doing one thing, my mind is badgering me to get on and do the next thing. I feel under pressure. I feel that I do not have enough time to do all the actions correctly. Consequently, on completion, I often find that the job has not been done well.

Instead of a feeling of satisfaction, there is stress and tension. So, it is not just the speed of thoughts that is important, but the speed of thoughts relative to actions. If the speed of my thoughts (my instructions to myself) matches the speed with which I can do things, I will remain free from stress and tension and I will feel that there is time to do things properly. The effect of this is that I feel as though I am 'creating' time for myself.

Another advantage which immediately becomes apparent when this is practised is the ease with which actions and reactions can be controlled. Great sportsmen have control over their minds when practising their sport, which is reflected in the control they have over their bodies. This is clearly visible with tennis champions. So precise are the instructions they give their bodies that each stroke seems effortless and totally economical. There is no wasted physical effort.

The spaces we leave when we slow our thoughts down allow us to change direction easily and immediately. When thoughts race, it's as though they gather momentum like a car going at full speed. If we are required to make an unexpected left turn, we then have to slam on the brakes, upsetting ourselves and the people in the cars behind us. We will probably overshoot the turning and have to waste time and effort, reversing and finally making the correct manoeuvre. When this happens in our minds, the emergency stop leaves us shaken and confused, and can be disturbing to those around us. However, the spaces between thoughts are like times when we are temporarily stationary. From a stationary position we can move in any direction we choose, smoothly and easily, without causing discomfort to anyone.

This practice of slowing thoughts down and giving ourselves more time is helpful in many ways. Above all, it allows us to be soul-conscious much more easily. Those spaces give us time to enjoy sweet feelings of peace and contentment, which are natural qualities of the soul. Then I can escape this physical world and fly to that timeless expanse, the soul world. This highest dimension is timeless, as there is no movement, just constant stillness. In my spiritual home I can learn how to slow my thoughts down to such an extent that they stop altogether and now, in total silence, stillness and contentment, I discover the beauty of eternity.

MEDITATION PRACTICE
Practise the habit of saying 'Past is past'. Keep facing forward. If something negative happens, don't feel guilty about it. Simply have the determination to conquer it. Re-channel the energy that usually goes into guilt or regret into positive thought and will power, so that the soul says: 'Yes, I am making efforts to change and improve myself.'

THOUGHTS FOR MEDITATION

I experience myself as a bodiless being,... a source of light, peace and power in a world of light... I feel that everything is totally still,... timeless... Nothing is changing... There is the experience of deep contentment... There is nothing more that the soul desires... I am with God in my eternal home of silence... I absorb the Ocean of Peace... I remain with the unlimited source of all virtues and fill myself totally... I am overflowing with light and peace,... spreading the qualities of the Supreme into this world...

Lesson 9
The eight powers

E ight powers are specifically mentioned as being developed through Raja Yoga. At first they might seem like eight qualities, but the word 'power' has been used, in this context, for a particular reason. What is the difference between a quality and a power? A quality is something which others can sometimes see in us, but it is also sometimes hidden. It is something which others appreciate, but do not necessarily feel that they can possess. A power is something that cannot remain hidden; it is a constant source of inspiration to others so that they too can change themselves and become powerful.

The eight powers are – to WITHDRAW thoughts, to PACK UP waste thoughts, to DISCRIMINATE best options, to JUDGE beneficial from harmful, to TOLERATE behaviour, ACCOMMODATE variety tastes or desires, to FACE obstacles (with courage) and to CO-OPERATE with everyone.

It is important not just to know what these powers are, but even more important to understand when and how to use them. For instance, if I am constantly tolerating someone's bad behaviour and the situation is getting steadily worse, perhaps I should really be using the power to face, that is, to have courage, and say, in a peaceful but firm way, that such behaviour is not acceptable. The eight powers are such that in any situation there will be at least one power that is appropriate for my use. The correct choice of that power will depend on my remaining calm and having a clear picture of the situation in question.

1) THE POWER TO WITHDRAW my thoughts is possible, even while I act. Naturally my thoughts must also be involved, but during any task, I can withdraw every so often and practise returning to my state of inner peace. In this way my thoughts do not continue to be involved when not absolutely necessary and I waste no mental effort. This is true controlling power which brings great strength to the soul.

2) THE POWER TO PACK UP waste thoughts in soul-consciousness means that I can 'travel light', packing only that which is necessary. Not carrying around negative and wasteful thoughts keeps me free from both mental and physical tiredness. This economy brings power and a completely positive outlook.

3) THE POWER TO DISCRIMINATE is the ability to give the correct values to the thoughts, words and actions of myself and others. Just as the jeweller can discriminate false from real

diamonds, so I should be able to keep positive, worthwhile thoughts and discard negative, harmful ones. It is the negative thoughts which often cloud true discrimination and I am eliminating these through meditation.

4) THE POWER TO JUDGE allows me to make clear, quick, accurate and unbiased decisions. For this I need to be above the influence of situations and the emotions and opinions of others. I also need a clear understanding of what is right and wrong. Raja Yoga meditation provides this strength and clarity of the intellect through greater self-understanding and a detached perspective.

5) THE POWER TO TOLERATE difficulties involves the ability to go beyond the influence of negative situations, to be able not to react, even in thoughts. If someone offers me insults, criticism or anger, or if there is physical suffering, with the power to tolerate I can remain peaceful and happy. On the basis of soul-consciousness, I will be able to give love, like the fruit tree which, when pelted with sticks and stones, gives its fruit in return.

6) THE POWER TO ACCOMMODATE is the power to be above any clash of personality or nature, to be able to mould and adjust myself, as the situation requires. I should not be one to create conflict in any situation. Just as an ocean can accommodate all the rivers flowing into it, so I should not reject anyone or anything. Instead, I am able to change relationships and circumstances through the power of good wishes.

7) THE POWER TO FACE obstacles in life is developed by meditation, through which I experience my original nature of peace

and become detached from the consciousness of the physical costume. I am then able to observe and see beyond problems and difficulties, to discover a positive side to something which seems totally negative; this gives me the strength to face situations.

8) THE POWER TO CO-OPERATE with others requires the vision of soul-consciousness, with which I can see all as my brothers and sisters. This attitude of brotherly vision creates unity and strength within a group. This power of co-operation will make any task seem easy.

These eight powers become more and more effective in my life as I become expert in applying them to situations, as required.

In conclusion

This small book provides a brief introduction to the concepts underlying the study and practice of Raja Yoga meditation. After having read this book, it is important to clarify the process by which you can use this information in a personally meaningful and satisfying way. The aim of Raja Yoga is to provide a means by which you can become the master of your own mind and your own destiny, and thus acquire constant peace of mind. So, it is essential for you to proceed at your own pace in a way which feels comfortable. Above all else, you need to develop faith in yourself.

Having faith in yourself means having the courage to explore what you are capable of experiencing. Blind faith is not a reliable foundation. If one places trust in things that are not understood, sooner or later that trust is going to be shattered. Firstly, there must be understanding; for this, knowledge is needed. In Raja Yoga very specific knowledge is given. Think about this knowledge, understand it and develop a clear picture in your mind. Think about the implications of being a pure, peaceful soul. What effect will it have on your practical life?... How will it affect your relationships with others?... Does the Law of Karma provide adequate explanations of current situations in your life and in the world?... If God exists, will it be possible to have a relationship with Him?... Only if you consider the implications of the knowledge are you going to have some sort of measure, against which to place the practical experience of meditation and daily interactions.

When you sit in yoga you can see if your experience matches up to the information you have been given. If you practise soul-consciousness during the day, you can see if this brings the results predicted by the knowledge. There will then be a basis for faith; it will rest on the firm foundation of your own experience, not only in meditation, but in practical life also.

Faith needs an aim. To measure your progress, you need to know where you have come from and where you want to go. Knowing where you have come from is not difficult; knowing where you want to go is more subtle. Knowledge tells you, 'I am a peaceful soul', or 'Om shanti', but how do you translate this into experience? Deep inside you desire peace but it is like a half-forgotten memory. That desire for peace is being prompted by a sanskara, a sanskara telling you that you must have had an experience of very deep peace before. You are not aiming for something you have never known before. Your aim is simply to rediscover that forgotten feeling of being so peaceful that you are ever-content. When you experience peace in meditation, it feels so natural and easy. It is an effortless thing. Your aim is to be in that experience constantly. Whatever you are doing, whoever you are speaking to, whatever is happening around you, you remain 'Om shanti', lost in the ocean of peace, spreading vibrations of peace to others. Faith needs both understanding and experience to sustain it. So, simply make sure that you combine ongoing study of this knowledge with the practical experience of meditation. In this way your life becomes an inspiring source of positivity and happiness for yourself and for those with whom you interact.

Om shanti

Other Eternity Ink meditation books, tapes and CDs available. For a catalogue contact:
Eernity Ink, 78 Alt Street Ashfield NSW Australia 2131
Tel +61 2 9990 7333 Fax +61 2 9799 3490
Email: indra@one.net.au
www.bkwsuau.com or www.bkwsu.com

Eternity Ink is publisher for the Brahma Kumaris World Spiritual University. If you wish to find out about the free meditation courses offered by the Brahma Kumaris World Spiritual University, contact the main centre closest to you:

UK: International Co-ordinating Office,
           65 Pound Lane, London, NW10 2HH, UK,
           Tel (20) 8727 3351
AUSTRALIA: 78 Alt Street, Ashfield, Sydney NSW 2131 Tel (2) 9716 7066
BRAZIL: R. Dona Germaine Burchard, 589 –
           Sao Paulo, SP 05014-010, Tel (11) 864 3694
HONG KONG: 17 Dragon Road, Causeway Bay,
           Tel (852) 2806 3008
INDIA: 25 New Rohtak Road, Karol Bagh,
           New Delhi, 1100055, Tel (11) 752 08516
KENYA: PO Box 12349, Maua Close, off Parklands Road, Westlands,
           Nairobi, Tel (2) 743 572
RUSSIA: 35, Prospect Andropova, Moscow 15487
           Tel (95) 112 51 28
USA: Global Harmony House, 46 South Middle Neck Road, NY 11021,
           Tel (516) 773 0971